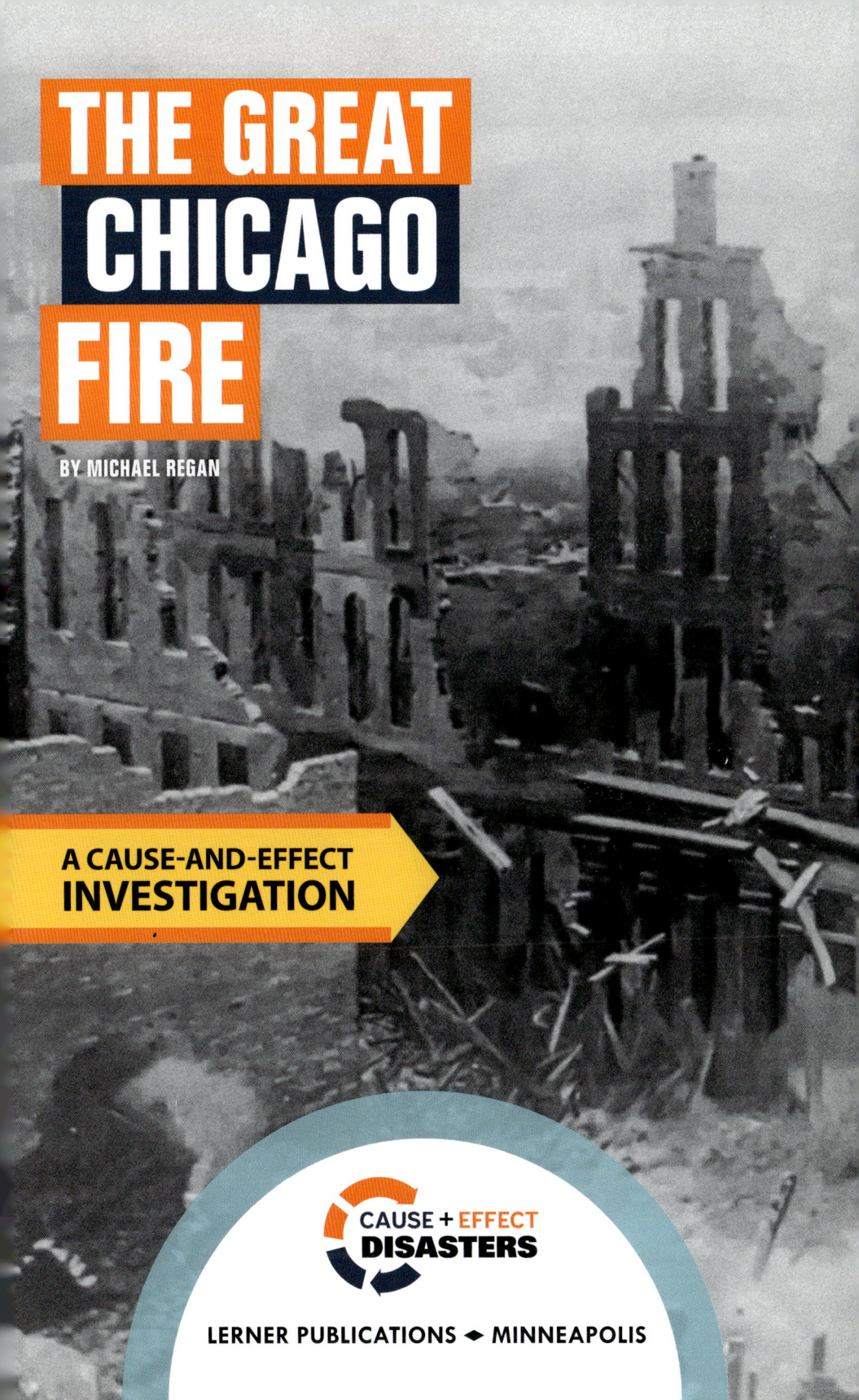

THE GREAT CHICAGO FIRE

BY MICHAEL REGAN

A CAUSE-AND-EFFECT INVESTIGATION

CAUSE + EFFECT DISASTERS

LERNER PUBLICATIONS ◆ MINNEAPOLIS

Copyright © 2017 by Lerner Publishing Group, Inc.

All rights reserved. International copyright secured. No part of this book may be reproduced, stored in a retrieval system, or transmitted in any form or by any means—electronic, mechanical, photocopying, recording, or otherwise—without the prior written permission of Lerner Publishing Group, Inc., except for the inclusion of brief quotations in an acknowledged review.

Lerner Publications Company
A division of Lerner Publishing Group, Inc.
241 First Avenue North
Minneapolis, MN 55401 USA

For reading levels and more information, look up this title at www.lernerbooks.com.

Content Consultant: Elaine Lewinnek, Professor of American Studies, California State University at Fullerton

Library of Congress Cataloging-in-Publication Data

Names: Regan, Michael, 1946– author.
Title: The great Chicago fire : a cause-and-effect investigation / by Michael Regan.
Description: Minneapolis : Lerner Publications, 2017. | Series: Cause-and-effect disasters | Includes bibliographical references and index. | Audience: Age 9–12. | Audience: Grade 4 to 6.
Identifiers: LCCN 2016008879 (print) | LCCN 2016009673 (ebook) | ISBN 9781512411201 (lb : alk. paper) | ISBN 9781512411300 (eb pdf)
Subjects: LCSH: Great Fire, Chicago, Ill., 1871—Juvenile literature. | Chicago (Ill.)—History—To 1875—Juvenile literature. | Fires—Illinois—Chicago—History—19th century—Juvenile literature.
Classification: LCC F548.42 .R44 2016 (print) | LCC F548.42 (ebook) | DDC 977.3/11041—dc23

LC record available at http://lccn.loc.gov/2016008879

Manufactured in the United States of America
1 – VP – 7/15/16

TABLE OF CONTENTS

Chapter 1
CHICAGO BEFORE THE FIRE 4

Chapter 2
A WOODEN CITY 12

Chapter 3
SPARKS FLY 20

Chapter 4
FROM THE ASHES 28

GLOSSARY 38

SOURCE NOTES 38

SELECTED BIBLIOGRAPHY 39

FURTHER INFORMATION 39

INDEX 40

CHICAGO BEFORE THE FIRE   1

Today, Chicago, Illinois, is a city known for its gleaming skyscrapers. But the city has a dark past. Those tall buildings might never have been built if not for a terrible disaster. The 1871 Great Chicago Fire was one of the worst city fires in American history.

Chicago's roots can be traced to 1803. That year, the US Army built Fort Dearborn on the south bank of the Chicago River. American Indians had already lived in the area for hundreds of years. Some of them had conflicts with the newly arriving settlers. By 1832 the army had driven most of the American Indians out.

American Indians were the first people to live in the area that became Chicago.

But some families and individuals stayed behind. They lived near and among the new settlers.

Chicago became a town in 1833. The population grew. In 1837 it became a city. At that time, the main branch of the Chicago River flowed east. It drained into Lake Michigan. The north and south branches flowed into the main branch. The city grew along the branches of the river. Buildings sprang up on the shores of Lake Michigan. The branching river divided Chicago into three divisions: the North, South, and West divisions.

Fort Dearborn, shown here in an 1856 illustration, was one of the first structures that settlers built in the Chicago area.

CHICAGO IN 1868
SOUTH BRANCH
NORTH BRANCH
MAIN BRANCH OF CHICAGO RIVER
LAKE MICHIGAN

Chicago was located between the busy East Coast and the expanding Far West of the United States. The city had access to rivers, lakes, and railroads to transport goods. Railroads brought grain to Chicago's South Side. It became the world's largest grain port. By 1871 more than twelve million bushels of wheat passed through Chicago each year. The expanding railroads also brought livestock to Chicago's meat processing plants. More than three million livestock, including cows, pigs, and sheep, were processed there in 1871. Chicago became known as the "Hog Butcher to the World."

Trains carried logs into Chicago from western forests. The city's many lumber mills stacked logs and finished wood products into large piles along both shores of the Chicago River's south branch. Chicago was also a manufacturing center. It had more than 1,100 factories in 1871. It was home to the largest farm equipment manufacturing company in the United States, the McCormick Reaper Works.

McCormick Reaper Works moved its business from rural Virginia to Chicago in 1847.

Boats docked at the piers on Lake Michigan. They carried lumber, grain, meat, and other goods to the East Coast. Those products were also carried through canals and rivers to the Mississippi River. From there, they traveled on to the middle and southern regions of the country. Some of those products were shipped across the seas to other countries. Boats brought goods from the East Coast back to Chicago. Some of those goods were sold in Chicago. Others were moved by trains and boats farther west and south.

Chicago's first train, called the *Pioneer*, arrived in the city in 1848.

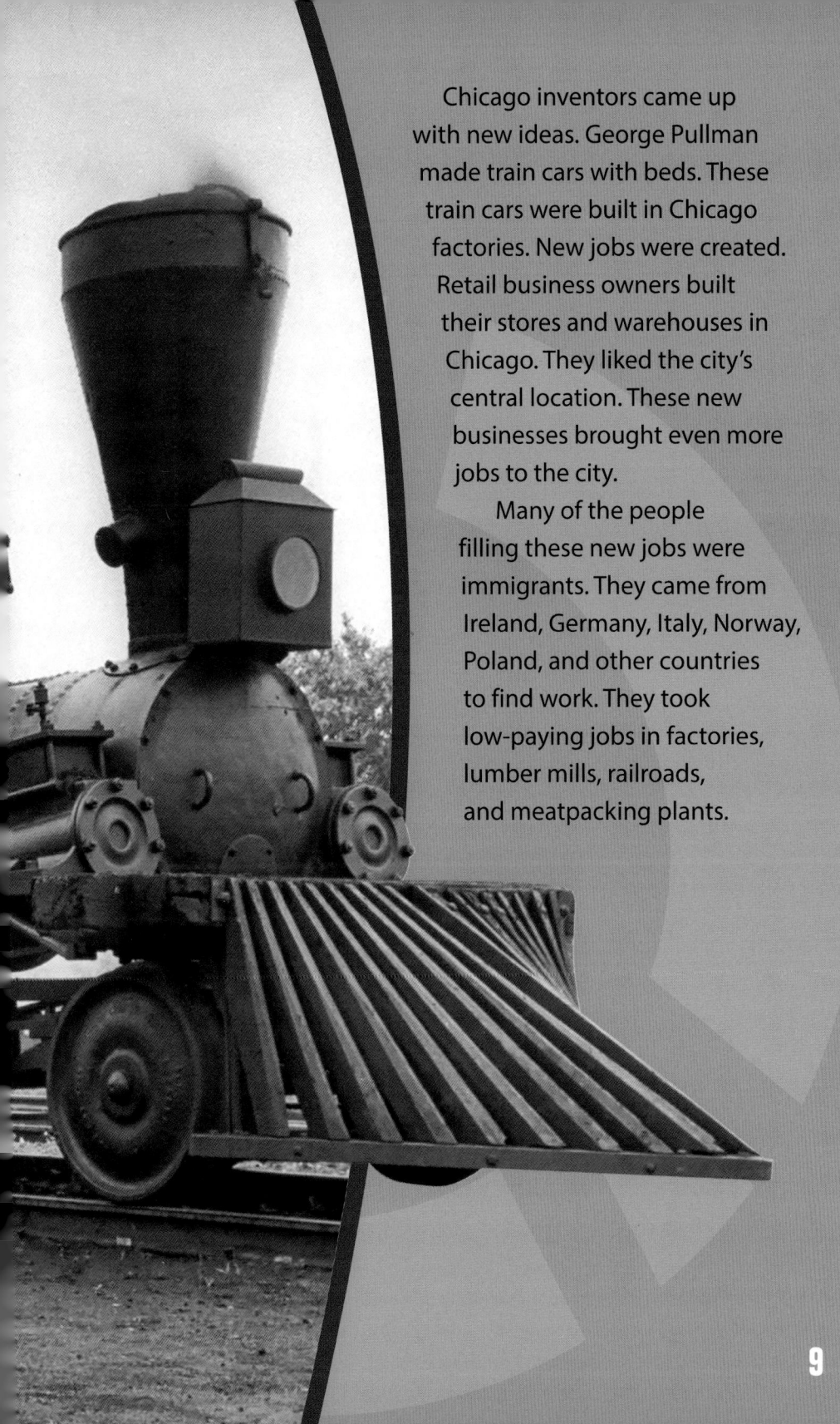

Chicago inventors came up with new ideas. George Pullman made train cars with beds. These train cars were built in Chicago factories. New jobs were created. Retail business owners built their stores and warehouses in Chicago. They liked the city's central location. These new businesses brought even more jobs to the city.

Many of the people filling these new jobs were immigrants. They came from Ireland, Germany, Italy, Norway, Poland, and other countries to find work. They took low-paying jobs in factories, lumber mills, railroads, and meatpacking plants.

About thirty thousand people lived in Chicago in 1854. By 1870 the population had ballooned to three hundred thousand. Chicago's many work opportunities were a major draw.

Chicago was a growing, bustling city. Like any big city, it suffered from minor building fires through the years. But soon Chicago residents would witness a fire unlike any they'd ever seen.

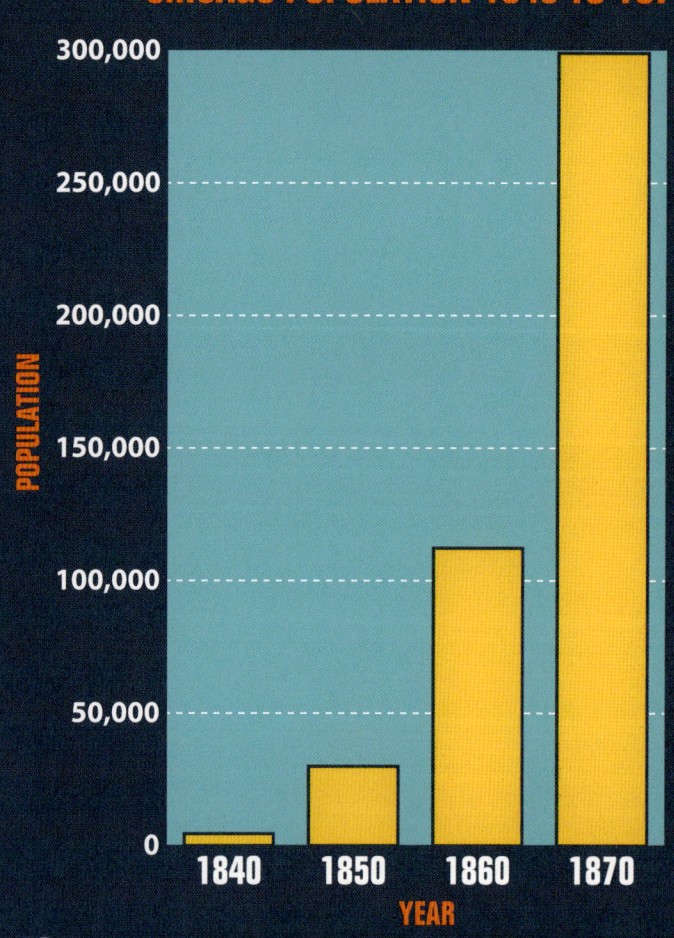

CHICAGO POPULATION 1840 TO 1870

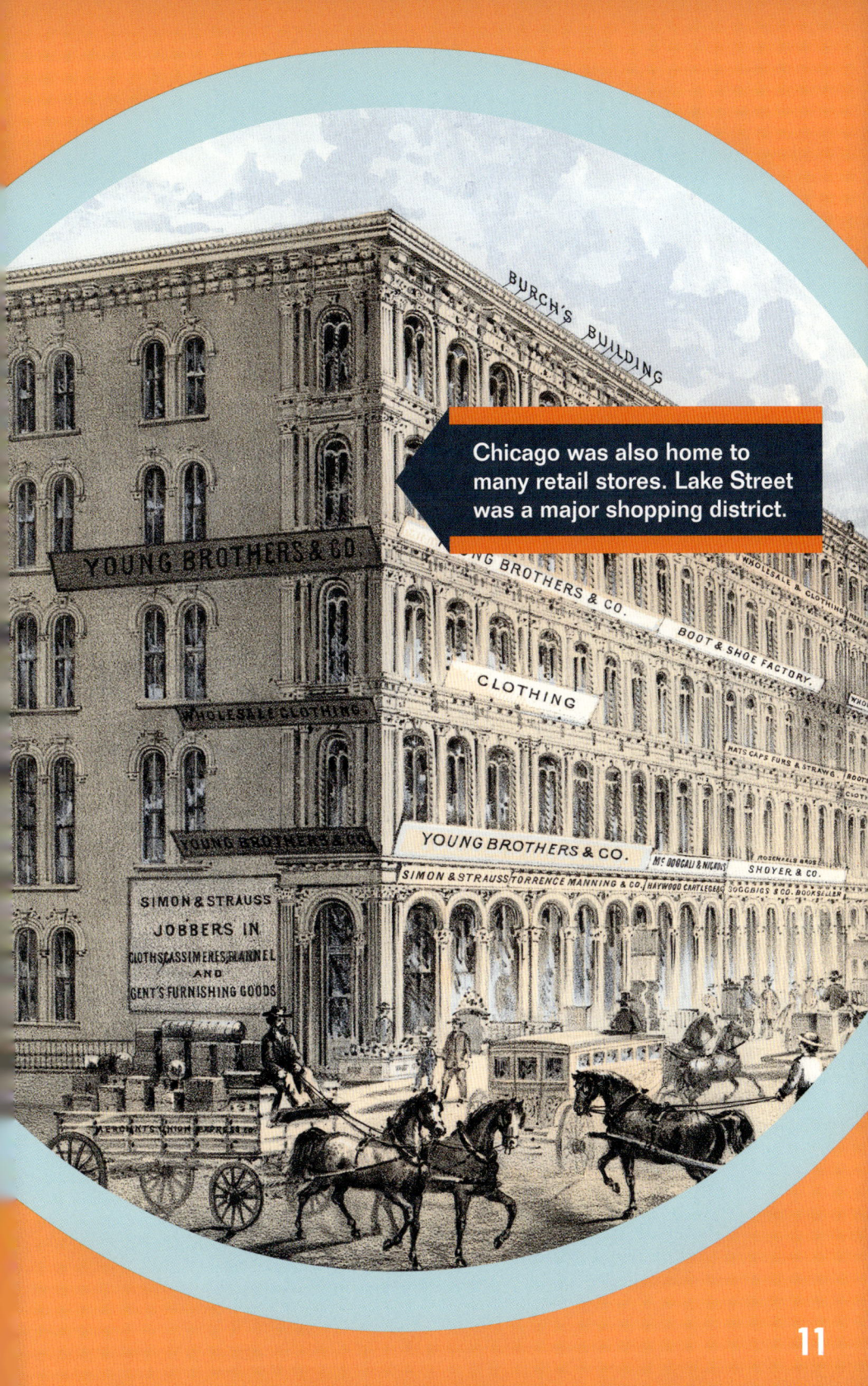

Chicago was also home to many retail stores. Lake Street was a major shopping district.

A WOODEN CITY

2

In 1871 Chicago had many modern services. The city had underground water, sewer, and gas lines. Chicago was the first North American city to build a large-scale sewer system. Fire hydrants and fire alarm boxes were placed throughout the city.

But old-fashioned building materials, the weather, and unheeded warnings made the city a fire risk.

From 1860 to 1870, Chicago's population exploded. Houses and other buildings were needed quickly. In the mid-1800s, lumber was easy to find. Building with wood was the fastest and cheapest method. Downtown office buildings might be covered with a thin layer of decorative brick. But they were otherwise constructed with wood. Only a few buildings, such as the county courthouse, were made of stone or solid brick. The roofs of most buildings were made of flammable wooden shingles and tar. The city's waterworks building in the North Division had a fireproof slate roof. But the structure itself was wood.

The county courthouse and city hall, completed in 1853, contained the mayor's quarters, the jail, and courtrooms, among other offices.

Chicago real-estate developer Potter Palmer built homes such as this one in the late 1860s and early 1870s. Many were constructed of wood.

Many immigrant workers were poor. They could not afford expensive homes. To save money, two or more families might share a small wooden house. Others rented rooms in cramped wooden apartment buildings. Those buildings were packed closely together. Some were built close to the city gasworks and the main downtown business area of South Chicago. Others were located around lumber mills and factories. People with more money built stone houses on the edges of Chicago. Or they built large wooden mansions in less crowded areas of the city.

Even the streets were made with wood. Chicago was built on muddy, soggy land along the edges of the Chicago River and Lake Michigan. Roads were paved to keep horse-drawn wagons from getting stuck in the mud. Some streets were paved with stone. But 57 miles (92 kilometers) of those roads were paved in wood. Chicago also had 561 miles (903 km) of wooden

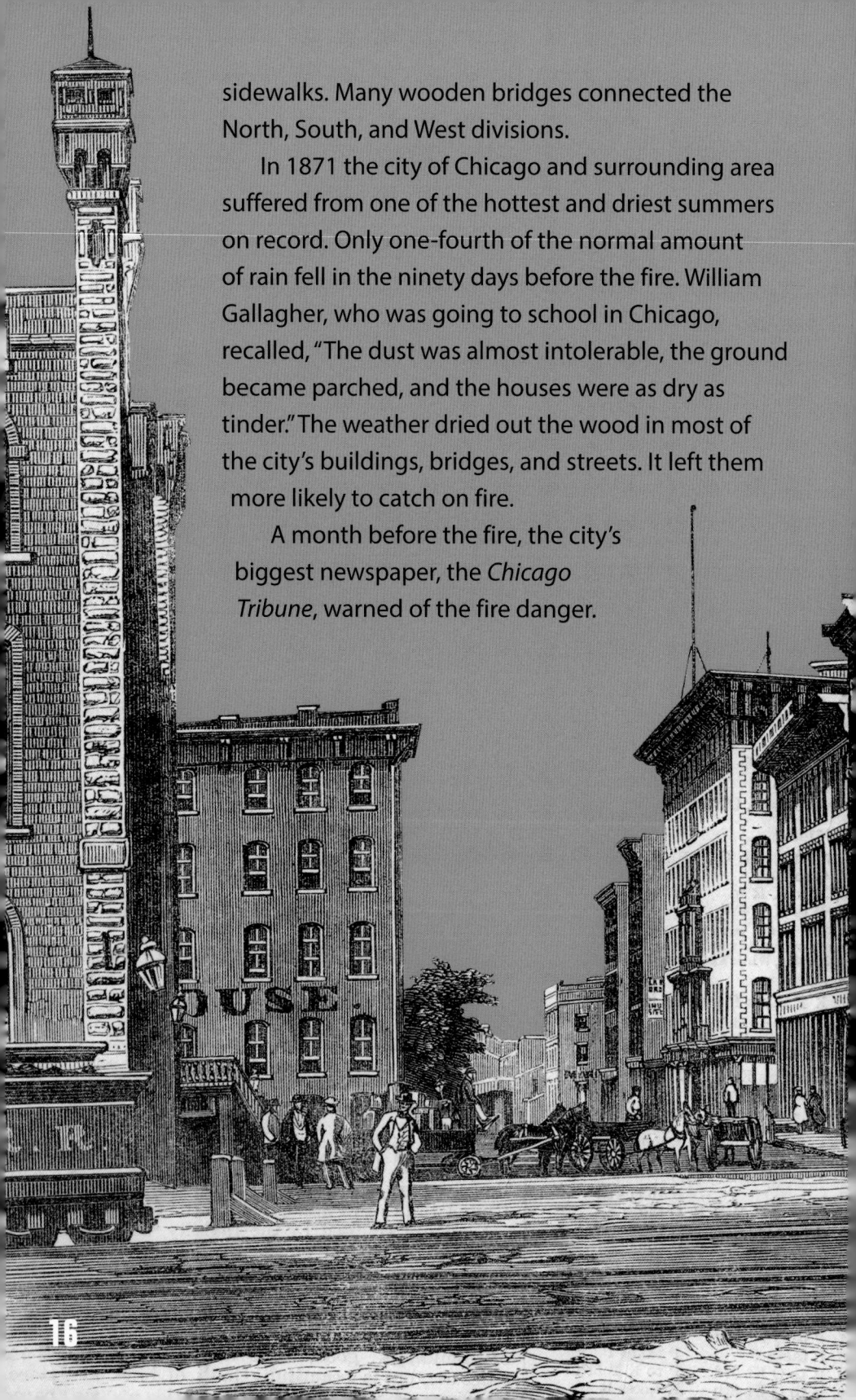

sidewalks. Many wooden bridges connected the North, South, and West divisions.

In 1871 the city of Chicago and surrounding area suffered from one of the hottest and driest summers on record. Only one-fourth of the normal amount of rain fell in the ninety days before the fire. William Gallagher, who was going to school in Chicago, recalled, "The dust was almost intolerable, the ground became parched, and the houses were as dry as tinder." The weather dried out the wood in most of the city's buildings, bridges, and streets. It left them more likely to catch on fire.

A month before the fire, the city's biggest newspaper, the *Chicago Tribune*, warned of the fire danger.

The Chicago fire department had been concerned for years. It warned builders not to build houses and apartments too close together. It also warned against using wooden shingles and flammable tar on roofs. But many homebuilders and apartment owners could afford only wood.

The fire department asked the city to start a building inspection program. It wanted unsafe buildings torn down. It wanted to replace them with safer, fire-resistant buildings. The fire department also asked for more fire hydrants. It asked for better firefighting equipment, including

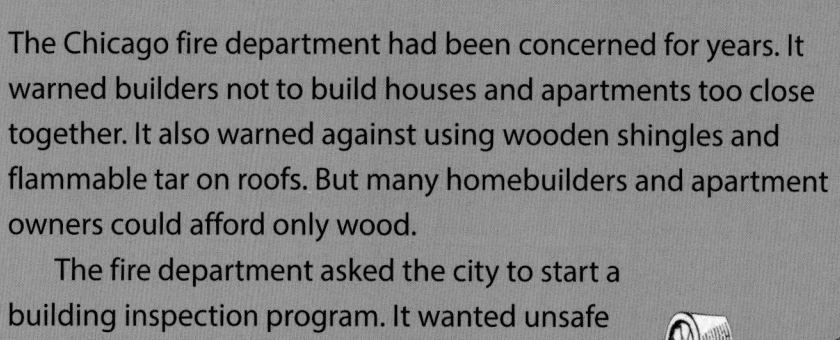

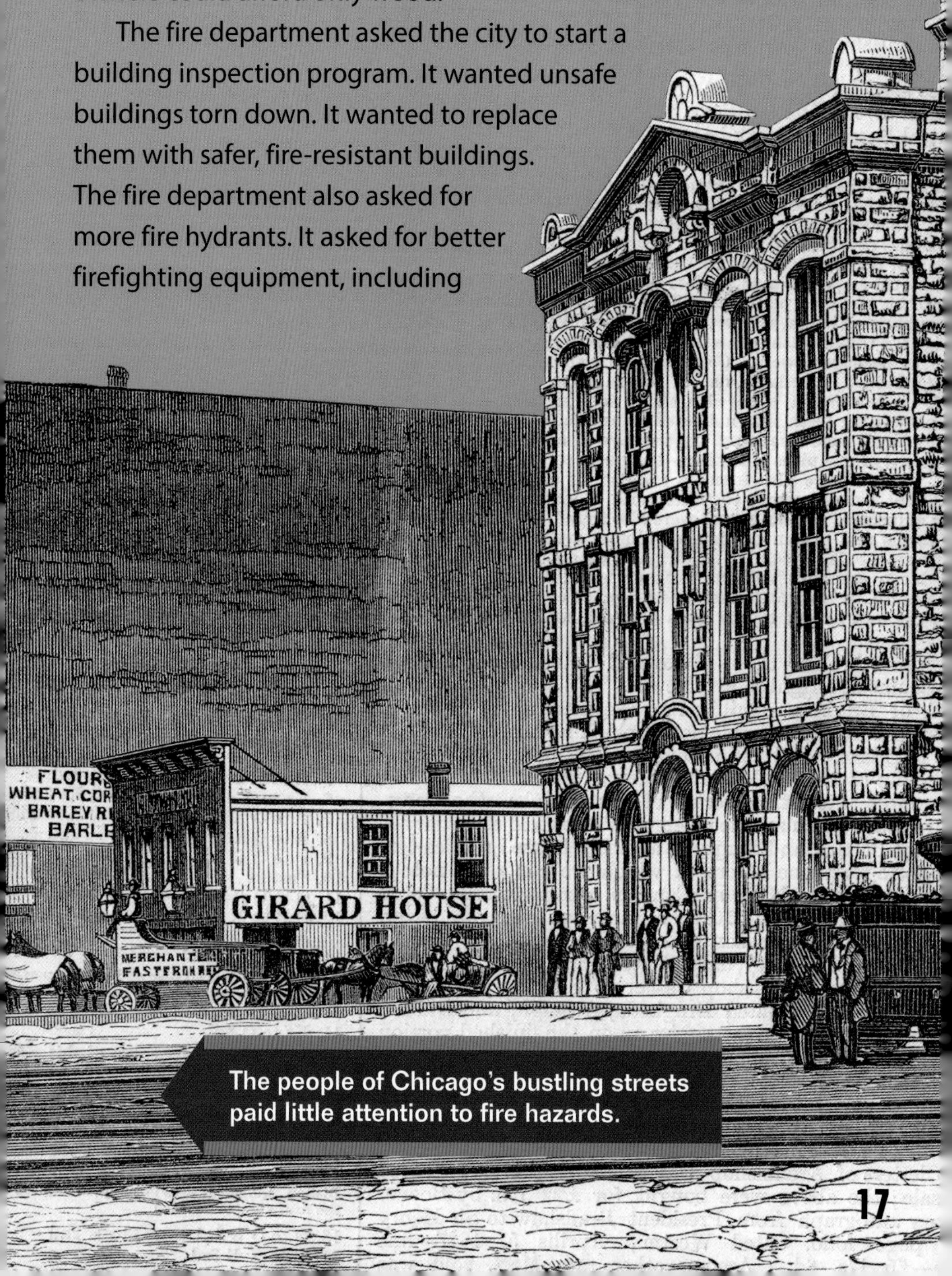

The people of Chicago's bustling streets paid little attention to fire hazards.

fireboats. But the city turned down all of these requests. They wanted to keep taxes low. Low taxes would attract more businesses to Chicago.

Chicago was one of the first cities to have a professional fire department. But at the time of the Great Fire, Chicago had only 193 paid firefighters. This was not nearly enough for a city of more than three hundred thousand people.

In the week leading up to the fire, the Chicago fire department had already fought twenty fires. The day of the Great Fire, many firefighters had just finished a seventeen-hour shift. They had been fighting a fire in a lumber mill. They'd had less than six hours rest. In addition, three of the fire department's seventeen fire engines were not working. On Sunday, October 8, 1871, the department was ill prepared to deal with another fire.

The Chicago fire department wanted fireboats such this one to help control fires near the waterfront.

Firefighters of the late 1800s wore leather helmets and heavy wool uniforms. Wool is naturally fire resistant.

SPARKS FLY 3

According to legend, the Great Chicago Fire began when Mrs. O'Leary's cow kicked over a lantern in her barn. Newspaper reporters later admitted they made up the story about the cow. But experts agreed the fire started in or near the O'Learys' barn at about 8:30 p.m. on Sunday, October 8, 1871. No one knows

After reporters created the story about Mrs. O'Leary's cow, the tale spread.

why the O'Learys and their neighbors did not use the firebox alarm at the end of their street. They did not run to alert the firefighters at the firehouse only six blocks away, either. They stood and watched as the fire leaped from house to house.

At approximately nine o'clock that night a fire department lookout spotted the blaze at the O'Leary barn. He had a map of the whole city. The map divided the city into sections called grids. The lookout gave the wrong grid location to the fire-engine dispatcher. The lookout quickly realized his mistake. He told the dispatcher. But the dispatcher thought sending the correction would cause too much confusion. So, he didn't send it. As a result, firefighters first went to the wrong location. Meanwhile, the O'Leary fire spread.

By the time all the fire engines arrived, it had been at least thirty minutes since the first alarm. The fire had already spread to a church. Nearby barns and houses were also ablaze. The whole block was on fire.

The O'Leary barn was completely destroyed by the fire, but the house (*left*) survived.

The fire jumped the south branch of the Chicago River at 11:30 p.m.

Fire Chief Robert Williams called for two more fire stations to fight the fire. At around ten o'clock, strong winds blew sparks and burning embers to the northeast. They ignited an industrial area of lumberyards, wooden sheds, and coal piles. The growing fire headed toward the south branch of the Chicago River. This area had burned the previous night. Williams hoped these natural barriers would stop the fire.

The fire chief's hopes were dashed when, at about 11:30 p.m., the fire jumped the Chicago River. It began burning the business and government district in South Chicago. Around midnight, a thunderous explosion ripped the air. The Chicago gasworks—which provided natural gas to the city—had blown up. Gas powered all lights in the area. The city went dark. Glowing flames provided the only light.

People streamed out of their houses to escape the oncoming fire. As the fire grew, the rising hot air sucked in cooler air. It created a "fire tornado." The fire tornado swirled high into the sky. It carried burning embers. The resulting firestorm spread fire throughout the city. Anna Higginson, the wife of a Chicago businessman, remembered, "The flames would dash themselves against the sides of a solid block, in one instant passing out through the other side [and] the whole just melted away [and] disappeared."

Even wooden buildings not touched by flames burst into fire from the intense heat. Metal spoons, screws, and other tools melted together. Marbles fused, forming colorful blobs. Brick and stone did

These marbles, melted by the fire, were found in the ruins.

not burn. But the mortar holding them together dissolved. These "fireproof" buildings crumbled to the ground. Most hotels, offices, and stores downtown, as well as the courthouse, were destroyed.

The inferno roared north. By two o'clock in the morning of October 9, it had jumped the main branch of the Chicago River. The North Division of Chicago was now burning. Residents had thought the river would stop the fire. But they now ran for their lives.

The city waterworks was on Chicago's North Side. At three o'clock in the morning it began burning. It stopped pumping water. Now firefighters had no water to fight the fire. They, too, joined the rush to flee the city.

People raced across the Randolph Street Bridge to escape the flames.

The advancing fire steadily closed off all escape routes to the west. People were forced to the banks of Lake Michigan. Once there, they waded into the cold water. This kept them safe from the flames and heat. Many took their horses and wagons with them.

On the city's South Side, where the business and government districts were located, the fire continued throughout October 9. Chicago's mayor, R. B. Mason, asked the US government to help keep the peace and prevent looting. Under General Philip Sheridan's command, US Army troops also fought the fire. They blew up South Division buildings in the path of the fire. This would stop the blaze by creating an open space between the fire and anything that could burn. This open space is called a firebreak.

In Chicago's North Division, the fire chased weary residents. People were forced farther north, beyond the city limits. Eight-year-old John Healy later said, "I saw a great sheet of flame descend on a frame building . . . leaving a bare burned spot where the house stood just minutes before."

That evening, long-awaited rain began to fall on the city. By early Tuesday morning, October 10, 1871, the progress of the fire had stopped. One-third of Chicago was left a smoking pile of rubble.

The fire left miles of buildings destroyed.

People camped alongside Lake Michigan after their homes were destroyed in the fire.

FROM THE ASHES

4

The Great Chicago Fire burned about 4 square miles (10 sq. km). This was about one-third of the city. Historians estimate that two hundred to three hundred people died in the fire. The bodies of many people were never found. Only 500 of the 13,800 homes, stores, factories, schools, churches, and saloons in the North Division survived. In the South Division, 3,650 buildings were destroyed. In total, about 17,450 structures burned. About a third of the city's population was left homeless. The fire caused $200 million in damage. That's about $3.9 billion in today's money.

Poor people suffered the most from the fire. Many were recent immigrants. The fire destroyed everything they owned. Their

jobs were gone. Their houses were burned. Many local insurance companies that insured these poorer neighborhoods went bankrupt. They could not pay for repairs either.

News of the fire spread quickly by telegraph. Photographers and newspaper artists arrived to record the devastation. People from across the nation and the world, including England and Germany, offered their help. Trainloads of aid poured into the city over undamaged railroad tracks. Food, money, clothing, blankets, tents, and medical supplies were donated. Mayor Mason issued a proclamation that the donations be turned over to the Chicago Relief and Aid Society. About $5 million was funneled through this private charity. Foreign donations totaled nearly $1 million. Even the president of the United States, Ulysses S. Grant, sent $1,000 of his own money for the relief effort.

Within a day after the fire, the aid society started its work. Many homeless

Men inspect the damage on the northwest corner of Washington Street and LaSalle Street.

people gathered at churches and schools for shelter. The aid society gave out food and clothes. The injured received medical care.

The aid society also paid for tools for carpenters and sewing machines for seamstresses. This helped people get back to work. Mary Kehoe, who was sixteen years old at the time of the fire, received aid. She recalled, "Anyone could get a new Singer sewing machine just for the asking. Food was brought every day." Many people were able to resume their work and earn money. Some people later complained that the aid society did not spend enough of the donated money it had collected. But the group had acted quickly. It was highly organized. It helped many people get back on their feet.

In November 1871 the city held an official investigation. It wanted to find out the causes of the fire. It decided that crowded wooden buildings, lax building inspections, and the underequipped fire department were to blame. The investigation

Newspapers all over the country reported on the Great Chicago Fire.

This cartoon, from the November 4, 1871, issue of *Harper's Weekly*, praises the generous donations from across the United States to help survivors of the fire.

report cleared Mrs. O'Leary of starting the fire. Mrs. O'Leary was in bed when the fire started in her barn. Still, many people and newspaper reports blamed her. The legend of her cow kicking over a lantern lasted into the late 1990s. In 1997, 102 years after her death, the Chicago City Council passed a resolution confirming Mrs. O'Leary's innocence.

Rebuilding began soon after the fire. The city gasworks and waterworks buildings were destroyed in the fire. But the underground water, sewer, and gas lines survived. This made rebuilding faster and easier. The fire did not burn most of the lumberyards, mills, and wharfs that lined the Chicago River. Many grain silos and meatpacking plants were also untouched by the fire. Their workers soon returned to their jobs. This helped keep the city stable.

Within a month, more than five thousand small, single-family, wooden houses had been built for the homeless. The Chicago Relief and Aid Society purchased wood for the houses. The aid society also funded wooden barracks for the homeless. Some city leaders thought all new buildings should be made of fireproof materials.

The Union Stock Yards were not damaged by the fire, which meant that employees could get back to work sooner.

But the thousands of people left homeless by the fire needed fast and cheap housing. In January 1872, angry laborers from the North Division protested at a city council meeting. They demanded that building with wood be allowed. City officials looked the other way as new wooden shanties were again packed closely together. Many businesses were also rebuilt with wood.

In 1874, only three years after the Great Chicago Fire, another large fire hit the city. It destroyed more than eight hundred of the new wooden shanties. Insurance companies didn't want to keep paying for burned buildings. They demanded that the city enforce its building codes.

Constructed in 1884, Chicago's Home Insurance Building was the first modern skyscraper.

Chicago was finally forced to change its ways. After 1874 it did not allow new wooden buildings to be built within the city limits, with the exception of some of the 1872 protesters' residential areas in the North Division.

Insurance companies also forced the city to improve the fire department. At the time of the Great Chicago Fire, the department had only 193 paid firefighters and 17 fire engines. By 1900 the number of firefighters had increased to 1,142. They had 5 fireboats, 101 steam engines, and 34 hook-and-ladder trucks.

Both good and bad results came from the changes. Many architects moved to Chicago to help design new buildings. The use of concrete, steel, terra cotta, and stone made buildings more fireproof. Enforced building codes made Chicago one of the most fireproof cities in the United States.

New steel-frame designs also made taller buildings possible. At the time of the fire, stone and cast-iron buildings could not be taller than eight to nine stories. If they were, they might collapse. The new, taller buildings were called skyscrapers. They could rise twenty stories or more. The first skyscrapers in the world were built in Chicago.

But the new building codes created more challenges for the poor and middle-class people in Chicago. Poor residents could not afford brick and stone to rebuild their homes. They also could not afford fire insurance. As laborers moved to Chicago for the growing number of jobs, landlords began raising rents for city apartments. Poor residents had to move out of the city. Many small business owners moved outside the city limits. There, they could build more affordable wooden structures.

Chicago's reconstruction eventually increased the city's size and population. Within nine years, the city's population grew from about 334,000 to 500,000. By 1890 Chicago had more than one million people. It became the second-largest city in the United States. As of 2016, Chicago was the third-largest city in the United States, after New York City and Los Angeles. The city prospered as a railroad, timber, meatpacking, and agricultural center. From the ashes, Chicago had grown into a major gateway to the westward expansion of the United States.

Today Chicago is famous for its skyline full of skyscrapers.

CAUSE

From 1860 to 1870, Chicago's population dramatically increased. The city needed more factories, buildings, and homes.

The summer of 1871 was extremely dry and hot in Chicago.

The Chicago fire department fought twenty fires in the week leading up to the Great Chicago Fire.

The fire caused more than $200 million in damage and took nearly three hundred lives.

Chicago building codes required the use of more fireproof materials such as concrete, steel, terra cotta, and stone.

Index

aid, 30–31, 32
American Indians, 4

building codes, 33, 34–35
building materials, 13, 17, 32, 33, 34

Chicago Relief and Aid Society, 30–31, 32
Chicago River, 4–5, 6, 14, 23, 25, 32

factories, 6, 9, 14, 29
fire department, 17–18, 22, 31, 34
firefighters, 18, 22, 25, 34
fire risk, 13, 16–18

fire tornado, 24
Fort Dearborn, 4

gasworks, 14, 23, 32
Grant, Ulysses S., 30

immigrants, 9, 14, 29

jobs, 9, 30, 32, 35

Mason, R. B., 26, 30
Michigan, Lake, 5, 7, 14, 26
Mississippi River, 7

North Division, 5, 13, 16, 25, 26, 29, 33, 34

O'Leary family, 21–22, 32

population, 5, 10, 13, 29, 35
Pullman, George, 9

Sheridan, Philip, 26
skyscrapers, 4, 34–35
South Division, 5, 6, 14, 16, 23, 26, 29

waterworks, 16, 25, 32
West Division, 5, 16
Williams, Robert, 23

Photo Credits

The images in this book are used with the permission of: G. M. Watson/Library of Congress, p. 1 [LC-USZ62-40297]; © Weerachai Khamfu/Shutterstock.com, pp. 3, 20–21 (background); Chicago Lithographing Co./Library of Congress, pp. 4–5 [LC-DIG-pga-03605]; Library of Congress, pp. 5 [LC-USZ62-35851], 22 [LC-USZ62-57060], 26 [LC-USZ62-40296], 31 [LC-USZ62-109591]; © Fuse/Thinkstock, p. 6; © Fotosearch/Getty Images, pp. 6–7; © Andreas Feininger/The LIFE Picture Collection/Getty Images, pp. 8–9; Red Line Editorial, pp. 10, 27; © Chicago History Museum/Getty Images, pp. 10–11, 12–13, 14–15, 20–21 (foreground), 24, 34; © Chronicle/Alamy Stock Photo, pp. 16–17; © Schenectady Museum/Hall of Electrical History Foundation/Corbis, p. 18; F. De B. Richards/Marian S. Carson Collection/Library of Congress, pp. 18–19 [LC-USZ62-122395]; © North Wind Picture Archives, pp. 23, 28–29; Currier & Ives/Library of Congress, pp. 24–25 [LC-USZC4-3936]; Melander & Henderson/Library of Congress, p. 30 [LC-USZ62-57045]; © provided courtesy HarpWeek, p. 32; Kelley & Chadwick/Library of Congress, p. 33 [LC-USZ62-97324]; © zrfphoto/iStock.com, p. 35.

Front Cover: © Weerachai Khamfu/Shutterstock.com, left; © North Wind Picture Archives, right.

Selected Bibliography

Abbott, Karen. "What (or Who) Caused the Great Chicago Fire?" *Smithsonian.com*. October 4, 2012. http://www.smithsonianmag.com/history/what-or-who-caused-the-great-chicago-fire-61481977/?no-ist.

Cook, Frederick Francis. "A Bird's Eye View of Pre-fire Chicago." *Bygone Days in Chicago*. Accessed February 25, 2016. http://www.greatchicagofire.org/birds-eye-view-of-pre-fire-chicago.

Hoffer, Peter Charles. *Seven Fires: The Urban Infernos that Reshaped America*. New York: Public Affairs, 2006.

Sawislak, Karen. *Smoldering City*. Chicago: University of Chicago Press, 1995.

Schons, Mary. "The Chicago Fire of 1871 and the 'Great Rebuilding.'" *National Geographic*. January 25, 2011. http://education.nationalgeographic.com/news/chicago-fire-1871-and-great-rebuilding.

Further Information

Books

Cleland, Joann. *Surviving the Great Chicago Fire*. Vero Beach, FL: Rourke, 2010. Discover the Great Chicago Fire through an informative graphic novel.

Cooper, Michael L. *Fighting Fire! Ten of the Deadliest Fires in American History and How We Fought Them*. New York: Henry Holt and Company, 2014. Read dramatic stories of how fires were fought, including the Great Chicago Fire.

Tarshis, Lauren. *I Survived #11: I Survived the Great Chicago Fire, 1871*. New York: Scholastic, 2015. Explore the Great Chicago Fire through a fictional story about a boy's struggle to survive it.

Websites

The Great Chicago Fire & The Web of Memory
http://www.greatchicagofire.org/great-chicago-fire
Explore pictures and eyewitness stories from the fire.

The Great Chicago Fire Festival
http://www.chicagofirefestival.com
Learn how Chicago's youth helped create a citywide Great Chicago Fire festival.

PBS: Chicago on Fire
http://www.pbs.org/wgbh/amex/chicago/maps/chicago_fire_text.html
Discover how and when the fire hit different areas of Chicago.

Glossary

barrack: a building used to house a large number of people
bushel: a measure of dry goods, such as wheat, equal to 64 US pints
code: a collection of laws
division: an area of a county or city
ember: a piece of burning wood or coal
firebreak: an open area created to stop the spread of fire
immigrant: a person who comes to live in a foreign country
industrial: a factory or manufacturing area
inferno: a large, out-of-control fire
loot: to steal or take
silo: a tower or pit used to store grain
terra cotta: brownish-red clay material
tornado: a violent rotating wind

Source Notes

16 "William Gallagher," *The Great Chicago Fire & The Web of Memory*, accessed February 26, 2016, http://www.greatchicagofire.org/anthology-of-fire-narratives/william-gallagher.

24 "Anna E. (Tyng) Higginson," *The Great Chicago Fire & The Web of Memory*, accessed February 26, 2016, http://www.greatchicagofire.org/anthology-of-fire-narratives/anna-e-tyng-higginson.

26 "Maps: Chicago On Fire," *Pbs.org*, accessed October 26, 2015, http://www.pbs.org/wgbh/amex/chicago/maps/chicago_fire_text.html.

31 "Mary Kehoe," *The Great Chicago Fire & The Web of Memory*, accessed February 26, 2016, http://www.greatchicagofire.org/anthology-of-fire-narratives/mary-kehoe.

EFFECT

→ Homes and buildings were constructed quickly out of the most available and affordable material: wood.

→ The weather dried out the wooden structures, increasing the risk of fire.

→ The firefighters were exhausted and low on resources. They were in no condition to fight the massive blaze that erupted on October 8.

→ Chicago created building codes to make the city more fireproof. The city also improved its fire department by adding firefighters and equipment.

→ Steel-frame designs made taller buildings possible, leading to the construction of the first skyscrapers.